Ozark Story-Poems

Ozark Story-Poems

Diane Taylor Denarski

August House Publishers, Inc.
LITTLE ROCK

Published by August House, Inc.,
P.O. Box 3223, Little Rock, Arkansas, 72203.
501-372-5450

Printed in the United States of America

10 9 8 7 6 5 4 3 2 1

LIBRARY OF CONGRESS CATALOGING-IN-PUBLICATION DATA
Denarski, Diane Taylor, 1952-
Ozark Story-Poems/Diane Taylor Denarski.–2nd ed.
p. cm.
1. Ozark Mountains Region–History–Poetry.
I. Title.
PS3570.A9272809   1993   93-9915
811'.54–dc20   CIP

First Published 1981 *Creek-Music: Ozark Mountain Ballads*, six new
poems added for present publication

ISBN 0-935304-30-4 (alk. paper): $7.95 pb

Executive: Ted Parkhurst
Editor: Jan Diemer
Cover design: Harvill-Ross Studios Ltd.
Cover Illustration: Jan Barger
Typography: Ira Hocut

This book is printed on archival-quality paper which meets the
guidelines for performance and durability of the Committee on
Production Guidelines for Book Longevity of the Council
on Library Resources.

AUGUST HOUSE, INC.   PUBLISHERS   LITTLE ROCK

To Debbie, who taught me courage;
To Cudjo, who taught me faith;
To Shasta, who taught me loyalty,
And to the lost one, Fuji, who
Taught me love.

Contents

Ballad of the One Dollar Mule

Grandpa was a Cherokee,
Indian proud and wild.
My Grandma was a lady;
A gentle woman-child.
When they were wed, they bought a farm
But Grandpa was no fool.
The rich dark earth was useless
Without a good, strong mule.

Now, back in nineteen-twenty-one,
A good mule's price was high,
So Grandpa walked to Holdenville
To see what he could buy.
Old Jack Simms had a wooden leg
And dollar bills to spare.
He traded mules and horses
But was very seldom fair.

Old Jack had a place roped off
Upon the village green,
And with him was the biggest mule
Grandpa had ever seen.
"Now, if yer lookin' fer a mule,"
The rascal cocked his head,
"This'un's the finest in the state!"
"How much?" my Grandpa said.

They parlayed for an hour and
A crowd soon gathered 'round.
The trader or the Cherokee
Would not be argued down.
Grandpa made his final offer and
The crowd let out a holler
When Jack gave up and sold
That army mule for just one dollar.

Well, Grandpa named his new mule Sarge
And rode home, proud as sin.
Grandma wept with joy when she
Saw Grandpa riding in.
Though it was nearly dinner time,
Grandpa just couldn't wait.
He hitched Sarge to the breaking plow
Down by the barn lot gate.

He plowed one row and then one more
In the field down by the creek.
Sarge never bucked or shied away;
Tears stained my Grandma's cheek.
"Oh, let me try it once," she said.
He smiled, "Well, what the heck?"
She placed her small hands on the plow—
The reins around her neck.

She clucked to Sarge and off they went
As pretty as a dream.
My Grandma and the army mule
Plowed slowly toward the stream.
When someone rang a dinner bell
Sarge stopped dead at the sound.
Then how that mule began to run,
Bouncing Grandma on the ground!

He bucked and kicked and ran like fire
Directly for the stream.
Grandma dug a crooked row
Then she began to scream!
Down the briar-studded bank
Slid Grandma and Old Sarge.
To people, dinner bells mean lunch—
To army mules, it's *Charge!*

Ballad of Sarah Raintree

They put me in an orphanage
And said I had to stay
Because my father disappeared
When Mama passed away.
Most people wanted little kids
And I was nearly ten.
They said I'd never find a home
Since I was Indian.

I tried to do the best I could
But everything I'd say
Or do was wrong, so one dark night,
I softly slipped away.
I headed to the mountains for
They'd known my mother's voice.
The wind and wolves were howling
But I knew I had no choice.

I told myself I'd stop to rest
When I got to the top,
But tears were freezing on my face
And I just had to stop.
The mountain night was bitter cold.
I knew that I was lost,
But I would never go back there
No matter what the cost.

I curled up by an oak tree
Where the snow was not so deep.
The storm sang lullabies to me–
I must have gone to sleep.
When suddenly, I heard a voice
As soft as summer air.
Before me was a woman with
Bright snowflakes in her hair.

She said, "Don't be afraid, my son.
Let's go home, where it's warm."
She wrapped me in a blanket and
We rode off through the storm.
I don't remember where it was,
But I can see it still;
Her weathered shack leaned up against
A dark, foreboding hill.

She sat me down beside the fire.
"There is no need to fear."
She bent down then and kissed my cheek;
"No one will harm you here."
She gave me something warm to eat
And sang soft lullabies.
Her voice flowed like a river and
I closed my weary eyes.

I woke up to morning sunshine.
I lay in a feather bed.
An old man smiled down at me,
"Son, we thought that you were dead.
I found you on the front porch in
The worst part of the storm.
It took both Ma and me to bring
You inside where it's warm."

I thanked them and I asked where was
The lady who had found
Me lying in the woods, almost
Frozen to the ground?
"Son, that was Sarah Raintree
Who found you in the snow.
She died while searching for her boy
Some forty years ago."

Ballad of the Phantom

Eagles rode WaPaTi's shoulders
And he spoke to bears at will.
In love with every living thing,
The young man would not kill.
People called him woman-hearted,
Though his brave soul knew no fear;
But, because he shamed his father,
He was turned into a deer.

They say, back in the Ozark hills,
The phantom buck runs free,
And his eyes are full of sorrow—
He was once a Cherokee.

As a child, I heard this legend.
We lived on a mountainside.
I inherited the homestead
When my dear grandfather died.
I left town in late October.
City life was full of pain.
I moved into Grandpa's cabin
With my little daughter, Jane.

I'd forgotten how, in autumn,
Trees rain scarlet fire-leaves;
And how frosty mountain breezes
Can sweep clean a heart that grieves.
Janie asked me for a story
Late one bleak November day.
As the wind moaned 'round the cabin,
I told her of WaPaTi.

It was bedtime when I finished.
"Is it really true?" she said.
Like a fool, I smiled, "Of course."
And then I put my girl to bed.
But, next morning, she was missing;
I went almost mad with fear
When I found her note, in crayon,
"I have gone to find the deer."

For, in the night, the autumn wind
Had turned a bitter cold;
And somewhere on that mountain was
My little five-year-old.
All my neighbors came to help me.
Widow Ingram found her bow;
But we had to stop at twilight
When the sky gave birth to snow.

I called her 'till my voice was gone.
I walked 'till almost lame,
When, in the midnight stillness, I
Heard Janie call my name.
The room was dark, but I heard her.
I stumbled outside to see;
Somewhere, deep in the mountain, my
Child called out for me.

A full moon watched above me,
Casting shadows on the ground,
When, from far away, she called me,
And I ran toward the sound.
On the dark side of the mountain,
Ankle deep in dusty snow,
I went in the direction her
Soft voice told me to go.

I ran blindly in the darkness,
Only slowing down to pray,
When I saw a soft light glowing
In some trees not far away.
Shining silver in the moonlight,
By my daughter's sleeping form,
I saw the great buck call me,
Lying still to keep her warm.

Frosty stars shone through his antlers
And I stared in disbelief
'Till I looked into his dark eyes,
Full of love and endless grief.
Slowly, he rose up above her;
Bent his head to touch her wrist,
But as I ran to embrace her—
He vanished in the mist.

They say, back in the Ozark hills,
A phantom buck runs free
And his eyes are full of sorrow—
He was once a Cherokee.

Secrets

'Way back in the Ozark mountains,
In the shadow of the sun,
Seth Maguire walked to the river
With a tow sack and a gun.
In the sack, a Redbone puppy
Shook with fear and softly whined,
But Seth could not afford to feed
A useless pup, born blind.

In the bushes, by the pathway,
Crouched a young boy, Matthew Winn.
He saw Seth Maguire upriver;
Saw him throw the tow sack in.
Matthew knew what Seth was doing.
So he waited, all alone,
For a pup nobody wanted—
For a dog to call his own.

Matthew's folks had nine more children.
They lived in a two-room shack.
Life is hard when you own nothing
But the rags upon your back.
And a young'un needs a puppy
Like an eagle needs the wind.
To the bowels of the river,
Matthew dove to save his friend.

Deep within a brushy hollow,
Matthew took the half-dead hound.
He had built a little lean-to
From some scraps that he had found.
And he named the puppy River;
Dried him off with rags and hay;
Fed him cornbread from his breakfast
That he'd safely stashed away.

Matt had never been so happy,
But he dared not show his joy
For his pa would call it stealin',
And his anger scared the boy.
So Matt kept his dog a secret,
But each evening he would go
To the shack where River waited
In the twilight's afterglow.

Matthew's dog grew strong, deep chested,
And, like Matthew, lean and tough.
Though they only had each other,
Somehow that was good enough,
'Till one evening, Matthew's father
Found the hidden lean-to shack.
He said Matthew stole the hound dog
And he'd have to take him back.

Matthew stood before his father;
Looked him squarely in the eye;
Told him how he'd saved the puppy
Seth Maguire had left to die.
But his father shouted at him
As the boy tried to be brave,
"I can barely feed you now, boy;
That dog wasn't yours to save.

You will go to Seth Maguire,
Give him back that stone-blind hound,
Then get home and do the milkin'—
Don't you make another sound!"
Boy and dog ran down the hillside
As dark shadows closed them in.
Ozark mountains keep their secrets—
They were never seen again.

Smooth Sailin'

The autumn moon,
Tied by the soft light
To the top of
My old pine,
Broke loose
And floated star deep
Across the sky,
Trailed by tugboat clouds.

Trespasser

I walked through the woods
On a cold winter day;
The dead earth beneath me;
The sky, a steel grey.
Bare limbs above me
Trembled with cold.
I walked and I listened
To words, ages old.
The bitter wind moaned
Through the deepening grey,
"You don't belong here—
Be on your way!"
I shivered and turned to
My home on the lake.
The woods became silent;
I started to shake.
My heart began pounding;
I ran through the gloom
But the dark, wrinkled shadows
Would not give me room—
And I heard, close behind me,
The screech of a gnome....
From the dead winter sky,
The wind followed me home.

The Calling

I know an autumn mountain
Softly veiled in calico
With a wild and shining river
For a ribbon, curled below.

At dusk, a she-wolf pauses
To sip the frosty air,
As misty eyed, the mountain
Lets down her auburn hair.

A shadow fox on silent paws,
His eyes like amber flint,
Comes ghosting to the creek to taste
Cold water, spiced with mint.

Come with me to my mountain
When the pain's too much to bear
And sorrow sears your spirit—
Close your eyes and meet me there.

Carolina Wren

She lived back up in the mountains.
Carolina was her name.
Her eyes were misty summer green,
Her hair was auburn flame.
Each young man in the village longed
To claim her for his own,
But her smiles were reflected in
The eyes of Jackson Stone.

Sing away the lonely night
Carolina Wren.
Bring my love and bring the light
Back to me again.

Carolina loved soft music.
Jackson's voice was warm and bright.
He would play his fiddle for her in
The moon-washed April night.
But one evening, when he kissed her,
She felt a small flame's growth
And, drunk on honeysuckled air,
The fire consumed them both.

Jackson promised that he loved her
And that true love was no sin.
She smiled softly when he called her
His "Carolina Wren."
He nailed two oak pegs in the wall
And hung his fiddle there.
He bought her pretty dresses
And ribbons for her hair.

The mountain learned their music
And crickets sang the tune
As newborn blossoms sighed beneath
An alabaster moon.
Carolina hated darkness
So, when evening would begin,
Jackson sang and played the story
Of the sunrise and the wren.

He told her that the sun grew weak
From shining bright and high,
And the animals were worried
That someday the sun would die.
And sure enough, one day it sank
Below the mountain's brow.
They had to bring it back to life
But none of them knew how.

When suddenly, from the darkness,
A liquid voice was heard.
How could such sweet, clear music
Come from such a little bird?
The tired sun grew curious
And raised up with a frown
And ever since, the tiny wren
Has sung the darkness down.

So all through that gentle summer
Carolina knew no fear.
Her laughter was a mountain creek,
Bubbling sweet and clear.
She was his Carolina Wren;
She could not ask for more,
'Till one day, down in the village,
He heard about the war.

She cried and begged him not to go
And kissed him once again.
He promised he'd be back in time
To hear their morning wren.
Now, back up in the mountains,
In a weathered, lonely shack,
She waits patiently in April
For a love that can't come back.

Sing away the lonely night
Carolina Wren.
Bring my love and bring the light
Back to me again.

Ballad of Whippoorwill John

Now, Sally Kincaid was a sprightly lass,
As gentle and kind as a fawn.
But she fell in love with a crazy man
By the name of Whippoorwill John.
Sally's pa owned the general store.
He had his retirement planned.
He'd found a rich banker from Fayetteville
And he promised him Sally's hand.

But every night, by the light of the stars,
While her pa was still a 'sleepin',
A whippoorwill cried from the mountainside
And Sally would go a 'creepin'.
She'd run like a fox down the mountain path
To the creek where John sat, grinnin'.
It's not my place to redden your face,
But they didn't call it sinnin'.

The banker got wind from a nosy friend
That Sally was carryin' on
With a mountain lad and it made him mad—
He went to find Whippoorwill John.
He huffed and puffed to the foot of the bluff
Where he'd been told they were meetin'.
He'd follow the trill of the whippoorwill
And give young John a beatin'!

But at dusky dark, a homing lark
Woke the banker from his slumber.
Then a whippoorwill from high on the hill
Sent him crashin' through the lumber!
He was whippoorwilled up and whippoorwilled down
And the cool air made him shiver.
He thought he was tough 'till he fell down the bluff
And was whippoorwilled into the river!

It must have been John a'carryin' on—
Is that what you've been thinkin?
Well friend, you're wrong, 'cause Sally and John
Were married while the banker was sinkin'!
How do I know it happened just so?
I've lived my life in this valley.
What's my name? I'll tell you the same—
My good friends call me Sally.

Widow Simpson's Ordeal

"The Lord is my shepherd; I shall not want."
Moonlight, filtered by pines, crept in through the
Window and shone down on the face
Of the feverish child.

"He maketh me to lie down in green pastures;
He leadeth me beside the still waters."
The mother's work-worn hands lay on a bible.
Her eyes were closed, but she did not sleep.

"He restoreth my soul; He leadeth me in
The paths of righteousness for His name's sake."
The child moaned, and as his mother bathed
Him with cool spring water, her tired lips moved.

"Yea, though I walk through the valley of the shadow
Of death, I will fear no evil, for Thou art with me;
Thy rod and staff they comfort me." Across the
Meadow, a bobcat screamed.

"Thou preparest a table before me in the presence of
Mine enemies. Thou anointist my head with oil. My
Cup runneth over." Covering her son, she sank wearily
Into an old rocking chair.

Once again, she closed her red-rimmed eyes. The
Child's breath was labored. His small face
Burned scarlet and he spoke to shadows.
There was no doctor but she was not alone.

"Surely goodness and mercy shall follow me all the
Days of my life and I will dwell in the house of
The Lord forever." All night, for three nights,
The rocker had creaked, back and forth, in the cabin.

At dawn, the child's breathing slowed and he lay
Still, at last. He slept. She brushed the silken
Hair from his damp brow as she tearfully prayed the rest—
"Amen."

Trial

"Misfit, misfit, won't conform!
Deviation from the norm!
Misfit now and misfit then—
Misfit's all you've ever been!"

I am neither fool nor freak nor liar.
I'm the one who set the moon on fire!
Listen to the river in my song;
Hear the mountains whisper, deep and strong!

"Misfit, we don't need your rhyme.
Mountains are not worth a dime.
Rivers come and rivers go;
That is all you need to know!"

But, I have meadow-music in my veins;
Forests richly spiced with autumn rains.
Taste my snow-crisp water, drink the air!
Tie sun-brilliant blossoms in your hair!

"Misfit, you must be insane.
Normal people don't like rain.
Plastic flowers don't draw bees;
Snow-crisp water makes us freeze."

Eagles-feather clouds across the sky—
Watch me. I can teach you how to fly!
Oh, if you could only understand
The joy of holding starlight in your hand!

"Misfit, we are tired of talking.
Pack your poetry—start walking!
Hop a plane or catch a bus.
You're not fit to live with us!"

I really didn't mean to cause you pain.
I'll just take back my mountains and my rain,
But, listen very carefully, my friend—
If I leave now, I won't be back again.

"Misfits, we've no need of them!
Wait, the sun is growing dim!
Everything is turning black;
Misfit, we were wrong—come back!"

Oh no, I am a misfit, tried and true
And I've no right to bother folks like you.
Afraid of darkness? I can't take the blame;
You lived in darkness long before I came.

The Way

Take only what is needed from the earth.
Remember to give thanks in all you do.
Pick up a stone and feel your own soul's worth.
Keep nothing that does not belong to you.

Follow the shining river of your mind.
Learn to speak the language of the wind.
In everything you do be strong but kind
And understand that death is not an end.

Vigil

She'll come upon you suddenly;
Her wings are frosty jet.
She speaks in owl whispers, but
I haven't heard her—yet.

The meadow knows she's coming;
His fear is emerald brown.
The wind is tired of waiting
And he blows the fire leaves down.

My whippoorwill down by the creek
Will softly disappear.
And early-morning mist will bring
The scent of death—and fear.

She'll grab fat summer by the neck
And shake him in her teeth.
His coffin will be sparkled air,
And marigolds, his wreath.

I know she can't be far away,
And soon, I'll hear her cry.
Her laughter is the music of
A lone goose, flyin' high.

Demon of the Ozarks

Long ago, I was a young'un.
Musta been thirteen or so,
When there came this old man walkin'.
Said his name was Ezra Noe.
And behind him was a young girl;
She was like a startled doe.
Lean and hungry, dirt-road weary
Was the green-eyed Linsay Noe.

Stay inside tonight, my friend.
That scream was not the wind.
Keep your fire burning bright
For the demon hunts tonight.

Her hand rested on the head of
A black, gigantic hound
As, up to us, Ezra strutted
And his dark eyes flicked around.
"I wonder if you folks could show
My girl and me the way
To the Stoner place; I won it
In a poker game last May."

Papa pointed to the mountain
And he said, "'Bout three miles back
Up that wagon road is what's left
Of the old Stoner shack."
The black dog right beside her,
Linsay stumbled out of sight,
But not a week had passed 'till
Folks heard screams up there at night.

Linsay wore her bonnet low to
Hide the marks upon her face
When she came to town. The black dog
Kept beside her, pace for pace.
Folks said back up in the mountain,
Old Ezra worked a still
And that when he drank he got mad—
Some say mad enough to kill.

Then, one dark October evenin',
Our young preacher, Robert Hall,
Went to visit pretty Linsay;
Just to help her, that was all.
Ezra, drunk, just went plumb crazy.
Said that Linsay was his wife,
And when Robert tried explainin',
Ezra swore he'd take his life.

Linsay's crying in the corner
Somehow angered Ezra Noe.
He picked up a fireplace poker
And he killed her with one blow!
Then he called upon the devil;
Robert spoke our good Lord's name
As the windows started rattling
And the door burst off its frame!

In the moonlight crouched a demon
Where the cabin door had been.
Eyes afire, long fangs gleaming,
Linsay's dog walked slowly in.
Blacker than a sinner's shadow,
The giant raised his head.
Ezra swung the bloodstained poker
Once—then twice—the dog lay dead!

All the preacher heard was laughter
As he stumbled down the trail.
Then behind him, in the shadows,
Rose a wild, unearthly wail!
When he staggered to the village
Crying "Murder!" in the night,
We all listened to his story,
For his hair was silver-white.

Ezra Noe just simply vanished.
We put Linsay in the ground.
Though we looked and looked, no trace
Of Linsay's dog was ever found.
But I've seen him, hunting, trailing,
Monstrous, ghostly head hung low.
Through eternity he's baying Ezra Noe ... Noe ... Noe...!

Stay inside tonight, my friend.
That scream was not the wind.
Keep your fire burning bright
For the demon hunts ... tonight!

Creek Music

They held a dance at the foot of my hill—
A Cardinal, a Quail and a Whippoorwill.
They flew invitations to each feathered friend;
"Music provided by Miss Lucy Wren."

Drinks would be served by "Friends of the Creek."
There'd be plenty of seeds for each hungry beak.
The dance would begin at a quarter of nine,
But by eight o'clock, they were standing in line.

Quintella Quail and Cardinal Le Roux were
Frantically wondering what to do,
When Whippoorwill John and Miss Lucy Wren
Opened the gates and let them in.

Horatio Hoot wore his speckled vest
And every bird looked his feathered best.
Bobby Blue Jay created a stir—
He said he had pecked old Farmer Brown's cur!

Each one applauded and offered a toast
For Bobby, they knew, had more courage than most.
They danced and sang on green grassy rugs,
Lit by lanterns of lightning bugs.

At moonrise, Miss Wren sang a goodnight song;
With Creek as a background the rest sang along.
I sat in the darkness beneath an old pine.
Though I wasn't invited, the pleasure was mine!

Dawn

"I will lift up mine eyes unto the hills
From whence cometh my help."
The sun reaches over the mountain,
Brushing away the night with azure flame.

"My help cometh from the Lord which made
Heaven and earth."
The eastern sky is afire, but the valley
Is dark and heavy with crickets and stars.

"He will not suffer thy foot to be moved.
He that keepeth the earth will not slumber."
The light on the mountaintop sets the trees
Ablaze and owls glide silently homeward.

"Behold, He that keepeth Israel shall not
Slumber or sleep."
The earth sighs as a gentle breeze wakes
The long grass, alive with quail.

"The Lord is thy keeper, the Lord is thy
Shade upon thy right hand."
A golden wave of light races shadows down
The mountain, surprising a late fox.

"The sun shall not smite thee by day
Nor the moon by night."
The reluctant moon watches sunbeams,
Tangled in the arms of the trees.

"The Lord shall preserve thee from all
Evil. He shall preserve thy soul.
The Lord shall preserve thy going out and
Coming in, from this time forth and even
Forevermore."

Hawk's Ballad

Long ago, before the white man
Came with paper lies and talks,
In the peaceful Ozark mountains
Lived a Cherokee named Hawk.
He was strong and quick as lightning
But gentle as the quail,
And the mountain was his brother;
He knew every hidden trail.

Redfern was the Chieftain's daughter,
And each evening she would go
To the creek below her village
Where small star-white flowers grow.
She would listen to the mountain
In her quiet, peaceful place.
'Till one evening, in the water,
She saw Hawk's reflected face.

For a moment she was frightened
But he begged her not to go.
He had only come for water—
Should he leave? She answered "No."
Being young and full of wonder,
Redfern asked him if he knew
Why the waters sang so sweetly,
And Hawk answered, "They see you."

She blushed softly in the twilight
As the young man spoke his heart.
Did she think that she could love him?
Redfern rose up with a start.
She ran swiftly up the footpath,
Shadowed smile and buckskin dress,
But the night breeze bore her answer
As she turned and whispered, "Yes!"

In the golden days that followed,
Redfern's heart was free of cares,
For her father gave his blessing
And ten Appaloosa mares.
But sometimes the sun is brightest
Just before the storm winds moan.
Dark Moon was an evil woman
And her powers were well known.

She had tried to make Hawk love her
With each potion she could find,
But she saw he loved another, and
Her rage destroyed her mind.
On the night before the wedding,
Dark Moon's chants were wicked, weird,
And when sunrise woke the village,
Hawk's young bride had disappeared!

Redfern's village was heartbroken
When no trace of her was found,
For at night, they heard Hawk calling,
And they trembled at the sound.
His brave heart was stone within him
And his step grew tired and slow,
'Till one day a village hunter
Told him of a fine young doe.

On the tiny star-white flowers
By the creek is where she lay.
There was something strange about her,
For she would not run away.
Hawk ran swiftly down the mountain,
But his heart was full of dread.
The doe lay softly panting as
He knelt beside her head.

Half the village followed after,
For they'd heard the hunter speak,
But they stepped back with a shiver
On the bank above the creek
When the doe began to whisper
As Hawk lay down by her side,
"I came back because I love you."
Then, she trembled once and died.

Hawk retreated to the mountains
In his agony and grief,
And they say the trees cried with him
And his tears stained every leaf.
So when autumn burns the Ozarks
To a brilliant calico,
If you see a shadow crying,
Calling to a moon-white doe
And the earth is bright with leaf tears
Falling, falling...
      you will know.

Humphrey the Hoot Owl

Humphrey the Hoot lived in a tree
Down by the edge of the creek.
His big orange eyes shone in the dark
Above his pointed beak.

He was a fat and fluffy owl.
His feathers were brown and gray.
He loved to fly and "hoot" all night,
And then he'd sleep all day.

His silent wings, each evening,
Would carry him far and wide,
Through the woods to the farms below
In the peaceful countryside.

Though Humphrey was a lonely owl,
He knew, when the time was right,
Someone would answer his plaintive cry,
So he "hooted" every night.

One evening, hope was almost gone.
He watched the lightning sky.
"Just one more hoot and I'll give up.
I'm so lonely, I could cry!"

He ruffled up and gave one "hoot,"
With tears running down his beak.
He turned to fly, then blinked his eye,
And Humphrey gave a shriek!

For there beside him, on the roof,
Was another fluffy owl.
She said, "Hey you, I'm lonely, too;
I want to be your pal!"

Now, they're as happy as they can be,
And they're really rather cute.
The lesson: You can have anything—
But, you've got to give a "hoot"!

Midsummer's Eve

Deep blue twilights, flecked with gold.
Bullfrogs sing by the swimmin' hole.
Honeysuckle flows 'round the Chinaberry tree
And the velvet air brings its scent to me.
The sweet, clear call of a whippoorwill
Sweeps from the valley and up the hill,
As an indigo sky, spangled with stars,
Drops light through the pines in silvery bars.
A new slice of moon, iridescent and clean,
Washes her glow in the mountain stream.
The old house sighs and floorboards squeak;
We learned long ago that she talks in her sleep.
There's a smell of rain in the breathless air
And we sit on the porch in our rocking chairs.
We talk and laugh, our voices low,
As a foxhound bays in the valley below.
The hour grows late and words are few
As we think of the things we have to do.
So, one by one, we end the day–
And a summer storm thunders the night away.

Medicine Show

Deep within the Ozark mountains,
In each little dirt road town,
Saturdays were when hill people
Came to lay their money down.
Merchants smiled and farmers squatted.
Womenfolk would spend their time
Pricing goods and sharing gossip,
Squeezing every hard-earned dime.
Every child could feel the magic
As he stood against the wall,
Staring at the candy counter—
Someday they would buy it all.
Then, down the road, they'd hear him,
Singing songs to say hello.
Through the trees they watched his rainbow-
Colored wagon, rolling slow.
Young'uns left the candy counter.
Folks stood staring at the rig
And the driver, dark and swarthy,
As he danced an Irish jig.
Close your eyes and you can see him—
Poet's voice and rascal's grin.
Taste the dust and feel the magic
Of the way it might have been...

"Mothers, fathers, sons and daughters,
Don't run and hide!
Little ducks on stormy waters ride—
Let it ride!
Worry will not solve your sadness;
Time's on your side.
Sorrow is the salt of gladness—
Ride, let it ride!

Does your stomach twitch and sputter?
Has your spouse lost all allure?
Does raw whiskey make you stutter?
I have the cure.
Dr. Christian Allgood's potion
Calms the soul, restores lost youth.
Harness cleaner, lady's lotion—
I speak the truth!
One large bottle costs a dollar.
Step right up, no time to waste!
Young man, you look like a scholar;
Here, have a taste.
Careful now, my lad, drink lightly.
Easy son, don't jump so high!
See, his eyes are shining brightly—
Now, who will buy?
Yes sir, you're this young man's father?
Can I help you out today?
Oh ... I see your badge. Don't bother.
I'm on my way."

Down the dusty road, still chanting,
Went the man who had no name.
(Oh, the sheriff's boy recovered,
But he never was the same.)

There's a bottle in the basement
That belonged to Grandpa Grant.
Dr. Christian Allgood's Potion,
Liniment and Medicant.
There's a little liquid in it.
Someone's tightly sealed the lid
But, someday, I just may taste it—
My father did.

Misplaced Melody

A blue jay sat down on the pasture gate,
Remarking to a wren who perched nearby,
"That cat Amelia's on the loose again
And she's got 'Blue Jay Special' in her eye."
A robin squawked, "This world is getting hard.
A bird can't make a living anymore.
Why, every dog and cat is on alert
And hints like that are too plain to ignore!"

Jenny Wren fluffed up and sighed a song.
"Oh yes, I know just what you mean," said she.
"My spouse left when the Health Department sprayed
The creek for bugs. Why can't they let us be?"
By now, a crowd had gathered on the oak
And every bird on every branch was mad.
The old tree fairly trembled with complaints
About the aggravations each bird had.

Then, through the April dusk, a cardinal came
And perched upon new grass of emerald green.
"I think that we should leave!" the blue jay screeched.
The cardinal, quietly began to preen.
A honeysuckle breeze swept off the stars.
"Hey cardinal," blue jay cried, "What do you say?"
A hush fell down upon them like the dew.
"Just give me one good reason we should stay!"

And, in the gentle April night, each bird
Found peace and understanding in one word
That somehow wouldn't sound right in a city–
The cardinal sang, "Pretty, pretty, pretty."

Morning Glory

In a dark deserted garden,
Choked with fern and muscadine,
Where the moss was emerald velvet
Grew a morning glory vine.
Long ago the garden flourished;
Every bloom was tinged with pride,
But the once resplendent flowers,
Long neglected, finally died.
Yet, the vine could still remember
How the garden used to be,
And she wished for some kind person
To appear and set them free.
But most people had forgotten.
They went blindly on their way.
"Who has time to tend a garden?"
Morning glory heard them say.
Soon, the forest crept in closer.
Heavy branches blocked the sun
And the morning glory witnessed
What the lack of love had done.
So she pulled herself up straighter;
Forced the weeds to give her room.
With a scrap of sun to guide her,
She bore one sky-brilliant bloom.
And a man, weary and ragged,
Watched the blossom burning bright.
Though his road was quite a long one,
He stopped there to spend the night.
He pulled back the death-dark branches
From the beauty, choked with weeds,
And the morning glory, shining,
Saw his hands were full of seeds.
Then her faith grew strong within her
When the sun shone down next day—
For one hand can save a garden
If someone will show the way.

The Mother

He ran up to the mountain when
His human mother died.
With open arms she took him in
And held him when he cried.
With cub and fawn, the young boy grew
Beneath a leafy dome.
Each fiber of his being knew
His mountain mother–Home.

Some people in the town below
Had seen him, acorn brown.
They thought him evil, wicked, so
With ropes they brought him down
As lightning fingers clawed the sky;
No longer would he roam.
And wind screamed from the mountain high,
"Beloved son, come home!"

They taught him how to read and write
And how to make things grow.
Then, when the war came, how to fight–
He volunteered to go.
Upon the mountaintop he lies,
Beneath the sandy loam
The Mother rocks him; rocks and sighs–
Her son, forever, home.

Mountain Music

If you think the best tunes are
Played by fiddle and guitar,
Well, who am I to say that you aren't right?
But I hear my melodies
When the wind touches the trees
And soft grasses sway in rhythm with the night.

When the sun has gone to bed
Every cricket lifts his head
And stars sing out in brilliant harmony.
When a hoot owl clicks his beak
In an oak down by the creek,
A full moon joins the mountain's symphony.

You can have your dancin' tunes
Played in nightclubs and saloons,
But I can't rest until I hear the song
Of quail and whippoorwill
When the evening breeze is still—
Maybe, someday, they will let me sing along.

Ozark Christmas

My Labrador had pups last night
Behind the kitchen stove
As dawn sought shelter from the wind
That cackled in the grove.

Dark limbs claw the window panes
While, from a brooding sky,
Heavy clouds weigh down the wings
Of wild geese, flying high.

Shadows from slow-burning logs
Contort across the floor
To mingle with their next of kin
That creep beside the door.

But peace is counting puppies
By lantern's smoky glow
And knowing that my gift has come—
A silent, silver snow.

Reincarnation

Whenever I close my eyes and dream,
I lie on the bank of a mountain stream.
The day is born as night grows old.
Dawn's light turns the water gold.
On the ground and above my head,
The wild things put themselves to bed.
I am tired and need to rest
So I make myself a mossy nest.
When twilight comes to end the day
Then I arise and stalk my prey.

Rememberance

The autumn buck stood drinking
From the icy mountain stream,
As ghostly morning mist swirled
'Round his image like a dream.
The fallen leaves along the bank
Burned scarlet, gold and red.
Standing still, I scarcely breathed
As the big buck raised his head.

He licked the drops of water
From his soft, black velvet nose.
He snorted once and sniffed the wind;
I gulped, just once, and froze.
His muley ears switched back and forth
Beneath the giant horns,
And then, his liquid eyes met mine
And stabbed me like two thorns.

The gentle face ten feet away
Showed something less than fear.
He snorted but my pounding heart
Was all that I could hear.
His wildness and his power made
My freckle face grow hot.
I longed to share his freedom—
And then, I heard the shot.

He flung his deep red body high
Into the autumn air.
He landed, twitching, in the creek—
I was no longer there.
I ran home fast as I could go
And each step brought a tear.
"What's wrong, Jody?" Mama said.
"What happened to you, dear?"

She held me as I told her and
She wiped my tears away.
Then she said it was my father
Who had shot the buck today.
As she explained, I understood,
Still, when the wild goose flies,
I recall the autumn of the buck–
And part of me still cries.

Request

Let me walk an autumn mountain
As she sets herself on fire.
Let me hear a full moon whisper
As she tunes the woodland choir.

Fill up my days with shadow deer,
My nights with whippoorwill,
And, perhaps, some fiddle music
For when the evening's still.

Let my earth-bound human heart
Thrill with an eagle's flight.
Let me glory in the power
Of a wolf song late at night.

I must tolerate the city
And I'll work from nine to five,
But I need an autumn mountain
To keep my soul alive.

The Saga of Sharon Moore

I used to watch the Ozark moon
Float upward to the stars
While tall trees fought to hold her down
With limbs like prison bars.
But, every time, the moon broke loose
And sailed on, proud and free,
To shine down, full, contented.
Something I could never be.

I thoroughly despised our farm!
All work and never play.
I longed to dance in city lights—
I longed to run away.
Will Parker bought a tract of land
The year I turned sixteen.
He was about the strangest man
That I had ever seen.

With cornshuck hair and hound-dog eyes
And cautious country smile,
He got to where he'd just drop by
And talk to Pa awhile.
But every now and then, he'd look
My way, like he could die.
Yet he would never speak to me
Until he said goodbye.

"Good night, Miss Sharon," he would blush
And shyly duck his head.
I'd smile if Mama poked me, but
I wished that he was dead.
Old country boy, that's all he was,
Just lookin' for a wife
To cook and clean for him—oh, no.
I did not want that life.

But Will kept coming, rain or shine,
And summer turned to fall.
Then, one day in late October,
I heard a stranger call.
A peddler stood beside our gate,
His knapsack in his hand
And mossy green eyes shone beneath
Thick hair as pale as sand.

I told him Pa shot peddlers if
He found out they'd come by
When I was all alone, like now—
The rascal winked an eye.
He said that he'd been everywhere,
Seen all there was to see,
But he had never met a girl
As beautiful as me.

I left a note for Mama;
"I will write you when I can,"
For that afternoon I ran off
With my green-eyed traveling man.
One year later I was pregnant
But he had the urge to roam
And I died of scarlet fever
On the weary road back home.

Mama cried when I was buried
Close beside a maple tree,
And I heard my papa sobbing
As he said goodbye to me.
Then they left me on the mountain
With an evening whippoorwill.
Sometime later I heard footsteps
Slowly coming up the hill.

Someone sat down by my graveside
And a voice, distraught with pain,
Said, "Good night to you, Miss Sharon,"
And his hot tears fell like rain.
William Parker never looked up
When the tree began to bend,
Moaning, stretching out to touch him—
William thought it was the wind.

Dilemma

I found a little tree frog caught
In my dog's water dish.
I said, "I'll get you out of there
If you'll grant me one wish."

He was so tired of swimming
In that dog-polluted sea
That he said, "I'll do the best I can
If you will set me free."

Now, wishes are expensive things
So I began to think.
I didn't hear my dog when
He came by to get a drink.

The summer sun grew hotter as
I thought of different things.
But I finally decided on
One dozen diamond rings.

I told him what I wanted and
Held out my eager hand
When I saw the frog, just sitting,
At the bottom of the pan.

"I could have died for all you cared!
Forget your diamond rings!
Your heart is full of greed, my girl.
You wished for the wrong things!"

I was amazed and couldn't think of
Words for my defense.
He hopped away and said, "Next time,
Just wish for common sense!"

Epitaph

Bury me beside swift water,
Mountain cold and valley deep.
Mourn me with soft fiddle music–
I will hear you where I sleep.

Let the summer fawn walk gently
On the grass that covers me.
If you do these things I ask
Then you will set my spirit free.

First Adventure

Suddenly, the woods were hushed.
She leaned over the dappled creek,
Entranced as her reflection
Shattered in the dancing water.
She bent closer,
Her long curls
Trailing in the swift current.
A young breeze
Ruffled her short skirt
As the baby willow tree
Dipped a toe
In the icy creek
And shivered
With glee.

Good Company

Dusty, gold drunkard
Kisses my country roses
Then flees, besotted.
Sun-scented fingers of wind
Brush through tangled grassy curls.

Tender leaf children
Wave at reflected sisters
In wrinkled water.
Bright minnows play hide and seek
With ragged shards of sunlight.

Not missing a word,
Old willow tree leans closer
To gossipy creek,
And I walk the dappled woods
With peace as my companion.

How Mustang River Got Its Name

Long ago, here in this valley,
Lived a man named Andrew Dyer,
And he owned a sorrel stallion
By the name of Shadow Fire.
Born and bred in old Kentucky,
Shadow's heritage was fame.
When that stallion ran for money,
All you saw was wind-swept flame.

Andrew's stallion was unbeaten
And his fame spread far and wide.
Andrew bragged that no horse living
Could match Shadow's flowing stride.
But, what good is a champion if
There's no one left to beat?
For, sometimes, to be unchallenged
Is its own kind of defeat.

So one day in late October,
Andrew spread the word around;
"To the horse that beats my stallion—
Who can run him in the ground,
I will give five hundred acres of
My richest bottomland,
And I'll put one thousand dollars
In the lucky winner's hand."

Andrew's offer tempted many.
Horsemen came from far away.
Pretty soon, this peaceful valley
Rang with hoofbeats, night and day.
Then one evening, she came riding
On a spotted mustang mare.
A black-eyed girl named Hannah,
With a feather in her hair.

She found Andrew in the tavern
Drinking whiskey, talking loud.
She said she'd accept his offer
And a roar went through the crowd.
"This young squaw must be plumb crazy.
Girl, what have you got to trade
If you lose?" Old Andrew chuckled.
Then she spoke. "Are you afraid?"

Samuel Jenkins was the sheriff
And he stood up with a grin.
"Andrew, you have had worse offers.
Race the squaw. You're bound to win."
So the race was set for morning.
Andrew woke up with a smile,
For he'd seen the spotted mustang–
That plug wouldn't last a mile.

Shadow Fire was prancing, ready,
But the girl was singing low
To the little spotted mustang
When the started shouted "Go!"
On the straight stretch by the river
Fire seemed to run alone,
But his body blocked the mustang
Whose swift strides could match his own.

Clear across the mile-wide valley
Eight hooves beat the deep grass down
And their thunder shook the mountain;
Andrew watched them with a frown.
Everyone was grim and quiet.
They could not believe their eyes,
When the stallion faltered, heaving,
And the crowd gasped in surprise.

Andrew stood up, then, and shouted,
But his anger was in vain
For the girl flew past the stallion,
Small hands wrapped in spotted mane.
All was lost. The race was over.
Andrew marveled at her skill.
Hannah's mustang made his stallion look
Like he was standing still.

She rode straight up to Andrew.
"Hannah is my Christian name.
This valley was my peoples' long
Before the white man came.
My mother's name was Windsong,
But you called her Caroline
On the night that she conceived me—
I've won only what was mine."

The Miracle

Deep within the dusty delta,
Where tall cottonwoods grow dense,
Grew a rosebush, wild and hidden
By a rusted barbed wire fence.
Weary farmers never saw it
As they toiled beneath the sun,
But a fox left red fur patches
Tangled in it where he'd run.

Summer honeysuckle choked.
Leaves were scarred by winter snows,
But within its tangled masses
Grew a late September rose.
One small bud against the wire
Struggled weakly to be born,
But the world she saw was frightening
And each fear became a thorn.

No one bothered to admire her
For the bush was thick and high.
No one cared enough to want her,
So they simply passed her by.
And the rose grew pale and weary
But her thorns grew sharp and strong,
For a rose without soft sunshine
Sings a melancholy song.

Then one day, the small rose trembled
Deep within her hiding place,
For a hand reached out and touched her;
Lifted up her dew-moist face.
And the one who held her gently,
Whose strong hand was ripped and torn
Was the one who saw true beauty—
And knew love was worth the thorns.

Night Watcher

My valley lies asleep beneath new snow.
Pale moonlight turns each flake to opal fire.
I sit and dream of twilights, long ago,
When bright stars lit a summer cricket choir.
But evergreens are frozen to the wind
And icy branches scratch my window pane.
I know how old trees feel when they must bend
Or break, and how they long for April rain.
The deer will come tonight while I'm asleep,
To eat the hay I've placed by frosted streams.
On charcoal paws, my Labrador will leap
Into the pond, but only in her dreams.
Alone upon this storm-scarred midnight knoll,
I guard the hidden summer in my soul.

An Old Man Speaks to Winter

As a daughter to her mother,
As a brother to a brother,
As one liar to another,
I can read your scheming mind.
If December days are sunny,
If the air is sweet as honey,
You can wager all your money—
Blizzards can't be far behind.

Since September, you've been waiting;
Plotting, planning, agitating,
Now your winds are desecrating
What was left of autumn's wreath.
So tonight, while folks are sleeping,
From the shadows, you'll come creeping
With the black north wind a'leaping,
You will bare your starry teeth.

While you're raging, I'll retire
Cozily beside my fire
As the hungry wind roars higher
With the wild moon in its clutch.
If my cabin starts to swaying,
You won't find this old man praying—
Why, it's just like I been saying,
Winter, you don't scare me ... much.

Legend of the Maverick Seed

On the west side of the farmhouse,
Someone planted one long row
Of the finest tall sunflowers–
Triple guaranteed to grow.
But a twilight cardinal spotted
One small seed upon the ground,
And he picked it up, announcing
To the world what he had found.

Sailing low above the pasture,
Arrogant and full of sass,
By mistake, he dropped the small seed
Deep into the tangled grass.
Lodged beneath a wild strawberry,
Sheltered by tall cattail shoots,
In her sun-warmed earthen cradle,
One small seed pushed out her roots.

Deep, green grasses held her steady,
Lullabied her in their shade,
Until she could cast her shadow,
All alone but unafraid.
Then one day, she rose above them,
Bowing gently to the sun,
And she saw her farmhouse sisters
Slowly dying, one by one.

For they had a house to lean on,
Pampered, petted since their birth;
Fertilized and shallow rooted,
They were strangers to the earth.
And the maverick flower trembled
'Till a flock of sparrows flew.
Powerless to help her sisters,
She knew what she had to do.

She sank each root even deeper,
And she grew to fill the need,
For she carried generations
Of strong mavericks in her seed.
So in time, beside the farmhouse,
Small ones reached up to the sky–
And the thankful maverick nodded
To each cardinal passing by.

Weaver's Folly

I remember Jesse Weaver.
He lived down on Crooked Creek.
Everybody thought him simple
For we seldom heard him speak,
But he had a way with critters,
Be it dog or mule or cow—
Like he knew what they were thinking;
Seemed unnatural, somehow.

He was known throughout the county
As an honest man and strong.
He'd work all day for a dollar.
Must be why it took so long
To save up that hundred dollars
That he sent to Colonel Green
Who had run an advertisement in
A farming magazine.

Now, the ad said "Quarter horses—
Finest bloodline anywhere."
And it showed a chestnut stallion
With his head high in the air.
Jesse kept that picture with him
In an old Prince Albert tin
And if you asked him about it,
He'd just duck his head and grin.

Then, one day, in early April,
I was walking into town
When I saw a large crowd standing
By the store of Simon Brown.
I saw Jesse in the middle,
Fighting for his self control,
Holding tightly to the lead rope
Of his hundred-dollar foal.

She was weak and spindle-legged.
Jesse clutched her to his chest
As the men grew breathless laughing
At the Colonel's cruel jest.
I pushed through the crowd and shouted,
"How on earth was he to know?
Leave him be!" Carl Jenkins hooted,
"Plant her, Jesse, she might grow!"

The tiny foal was shaking.
Jesse put her on the ground
And I noticed that the filly
Was no bigger than a hound.
Her brown coat was ragged, muddy;
She could scarcely lift her head.
They had called her Weaver's folly–
By tomorrow she'd be dead.

Rumors spread like honeysuckle
When old Jesse ran away.
But a little mountain magic
Can work miracles, they say.
In a cool, secluded hollow,
Jesse nursed the tiny foal.
She grew strong on meadow grasses
But pure love restored her soul.

I met Jesse one year later
Walking down a mountainside,
And behind him was a filly
Far too delicate to ride.
She wore neither rope or halter
As she danced along the slope.
I said, "Is this Weaver's Folly?"
Jesse smiled, "Her name is Hope."

Ballad of Fiddler Dan

I got lost up in the mountains
In a late October storm,
But an old man by a farmhouse
Bade me come in and get warm.
He offered me some coffee and
Inquired about my trade.
So I told him I wrote ballads
But was very seldom paid.

"I've a story you might fancy."
I could barely hear him say.
In the leaping firelight shadows
His blue eyes were far away.
"Mandy Brown lived in the village.
She was wild and fancy free
And it broke her mother's heart
When she took up with Dan DuPree.

Now, Dan played mountain music
Like no one had ever heard.
Why, he could make a fiddle sing
Just like a mockingbird.
High upon the midnight mountain,
Dan would play his fiddle low,
Softly calling Mandy to him—
And she never failed to go.

Jonah Small was slow and quiet
And he owned the general store.
If that girl had been an angel
He could not have loved her more.
Mandy laughed at Jonah's passion
And aggrieved the gentle man
By her taunting condemnation
And her love for Fiddler Dan.

Mandy gave herself too freely.
Fiddler Dan was just as wild
For, when he left town that autumn,
He left Mandy with a child.
As his baby grew inside her,
Mandy, sorry for her sin,
Begged forgiveness from her parents
But they wouldn't let her in.

Then one night, in later December,
Jonah found her at his door.
Nearly dead from cold and hunger,
She collapsed upon the floor.
He carried Mandy to his room
And in her pain, he cried.
Gently he brought forth her baby.
Mandy called for Dan—and died.

Jonah raised the child to manhood
With no help from anyone,
For the love he had for Mandy
Overflowed onto her son.
And the bond between them strengthened
Through the years, till Jonah died
With the fiddler's son who loved him
Like a father by his side."

When he finished with his story
I asked if he could recall
If the fiddler ever knew about
His son and Jonah Small.
He picked up a battered fiddle
As outside, the night wind rose,
And the old man, softly sobbing,
Cried, "He knows, oh yes, he knows!"

Stepping Out

Tonight, when no one's watching me,
Hand in hand with a scoundrel breeze,
I'll dance among tall fiddler trees,
My hair aglow with tangled stars
And dressed in soft, moon-silver bars,
I'll pause to sip cool fragrant wines
That cling to honeysuckle vines.
Upon a dark, forbidden hill,
I'll sing with every whippoorwill
And celebrate my being free—
Tonight, when no one's watching me.

Tomorrow, they will call me mad
And say that I've been very bad.
They'll dress me coffin formal then,
They'll ask me where I think I've been.
I'll hide the star caught in my hair
And tell them I've been everywhere!
They'll shout that lying is a sin
And lock me in my room. Again.

What fools to think that metal bars
Can banish breezes, hide the stars
Or keep a poet fool unfree....

Tonight. When no one's watching me.

Quill Creek

I know this place.
My roots are tangled deep with oak and pine.
The wild ones have no need to fear;
Like me, they've found a haven here.
If one can own a spirit, this is mine.
Branches touch my face.
I know this place.

I've tasted fear–
When orphan midnight squeaks the pasture gate,
Across the ridge, an old hound sings;
An owl swoops down on shadow-wings
And like a small, lost quail, I crouch and wait
For talon-spear.
I've tasted fear.

But light is grace.
While young things celebrate the passing night,
I've whippoorwills to sing to me
And wind to keep my spirit free
And peace that far surpasses human blight–
I've seen her face.
I know this place.

Ballad of Moccasin Annie

Herbert Creed lived back in the swamp
With Annie, his young daughter,
Where dark moccasins swam so thick
You could almost walk on the water.
Folks in our little bayou town
Whispered their names with a curse.
They said to look in Annie's eyes
Was asking for death—or worse.

Now, Annie's eyes burned witchy-gold;
Her hair was raven black.
Too beautiful for mortal man
But not for One-Eyed Jack.
He worked out on an oil rig
And, Lord, he loved a fight!
They say he lost his left eye in
An alley brawl one night.

The year that Annie turned sixteen
She started coming in
To town on Saturdays where she
Could mingle with the men
Who gathered for a friendly drink
At Crazy John's saloon.
Her voice was silk and honey and
Her eyes on fire with moon.

Now, all of us avoided her
But One-Eyed Jack was wild.
He got to where he'd slip off with
That dark and evil child.
She'd meet him by a live oak tree,
Her cat-eyes burning bright.
She waited like a panther in
The steamy bayou night.

Seems like, looking back, that summer
There were lots of snakes around.
Why, at night I'd hear them dropping
From the rooftop to the ground.
I was walking home one evening
Just this side of Haley's Pond,
When I spotted Annie standing
In some shadows just beyond.

I crossed myself and said a prayer.
Her eyes were glowing red.
Beside her coiled a moccasin—
She bent and kissed its head!
I knew I must be crazy for
The world began to spin—
That snake rose up to Annie's height
And kissed her back again!

Cold horror slithered up my spine;
Numb terror clawed my back.
Somehow, despite my trembling legs,
I must find One-Eyed Jack
And tell him, make him understand
That something evil crept
That night with mist and Spanish moss—
It waited while he slept.

Now, Jack had just got home himself
And he was none too proud
To see me standing on his porch
But, Lord, he laughed out loud
When I got finished telling him.
A twinkle touched his eye.
He said, "Boy, don't you worry;
I've done told that gal goodbye.

"I'm leaving in the morning for
A job at Willow Bend and
With any kind of luck at all,
I'll not be back again!"
The walk back home was eerie.
Every shadow seemed to creep
Around me as I walked along.
I knew I wouldn't sleep.

But fear will drain the strongest man
And, sometime after four,
I woke up from a nap to hear
A knock upon my door.
She stood there in the morning gloom
And chills crept up my back.
I couldn't help but tell her
What I'd heard from One-Eyed Jack.

Next morning, he had disappeared.
The law searched high and low.
Some folks still wonder where he went.
I wish I didn't know!
I've written this in time, I think.
I saw the snake tonight.
It slithers now upon my porch,
Its one eye silver white.

Cherokee Lullaby

My son, the earth you rest your head upon
Will love you ages after I am gone.
Your brothers are the eagle and the bear
And all of you must breathe the same sweet air.
The autumn moon is shining full and bright.
She watches every cub and fawn tonight.
So close your eyes, my son, and go to sleep.
There is no need to fear the ones that creep.

I saw you watch your father ride away
Upon his silver stallion yesterday.
You asked him for a horse to call your own.
"Someday," he said and rode off all alone.
But when he came back from the fort tonight,
Behind him was a pony, silver-white.
He took some woven blankets for a trade
And, when you run tomorrow to the glade
To feed the horses like you always do,
You'll find a special one tied there for you.
I know it's only foolish mother's pride
But somehow, son, I'll hate to see you ride.

The spirit in the sky will light a star
To lead you home if dreams take you too far.
But, just tonight, I'm glad you're here with me.
Be proud, my son. You are a Cherokee.

The Guardian

There's a place up in the Ozarks
By the name of Foley's Ridge,
Famous for its moonshine whiskey
And the Singing River Bridge.
Back in nineteen-twenty-seven,
On a steamy August night,
Near the bridge's south embankment,
Something slaughtered Ethan Wright.

Now, old Ethan was a loner,
But he'd never harmed a fly.
Oh, he'd made a little whiskey
Now and then, to get him by.
But the old man had no money
And no enemies, at least
No one mean enough to kill him.
All signs pointed to a beast.

On the white-hot morning after
Poor old Ethan Wright was found,
Folks were whispering about the
Giant pawprints someone found
Leading from the wooded hillside
To the riverbank and then
Circling old Ethan's body
Before vanishing again.

Johnny Reed lived in the mountains,
No one knew exactly where.
It was rumored he could change
Into a panther or a bear
Just by chanting incantations.
He was known to walk at night
Near the village—like the creature
That had murdered Ethan Wright.

Woody McAffee remembered
That young Johnny had a dog,
Far more timber wolf than redbone,
Fur as silver-gray as fog.
Selby's store was packed that morning.
All the menfolks were agreed
That, before the week had ended,
They would hang that Johnny Reed!

August in the Ozark mountains—
Rattlesnakes and whippoorwills
Shied away from angry footsteps
As the hunters combed the hills.
In late afternoon, the posse
Made their camp near Possum Gap.
Every man and boy sat, silent,
With his shotgun in his lap.

Mothers did the night chores early,
Gathered up their kids and then
Cabin doors were barred and bolted
As the shadows closed them in.
They tried not to think of Ethan
Who had died the night before,
Or of what was waiting, lurking,
In the dark outside each door.

No one saw the silent figures
Who came walking from the bridge.
No one saw them creeping slowly
Through the woods near Foley's Ridge,
Crossing meadows in the moonlight.
Crickets ceased their clacking whirr
At the young man's stealthy passage
And his beast with silver fur.

On the slope above the river,
Johnny paused to catch his breath.
He'd been passing here last evening
Just before old Ethan's death.
He had heard the savage snarling
And the old man's feeble cries;
He had seen the monstrous shadow
With the full moon in its eyes.

Johnny sat down on the hillside
With his arm around the beast,
Knowing that the Thing must kill
Before the sun rose in the east.
But his day had been a long one
And the silence was so deep
That, although he didn't mean to,
Johnny Reed fell fast asleep.

Something crept out from the bushes.
Something crawled onto the bridge
And its hollow head was pointed
At the town of Foley's Ridge.
Johnny's troubled sleep was shattered
By his beast's unearthly roar
As a Shape swept up toward them
From the river's sandy shore.

Johnny shook some golden powder
From a beaded deerskin pouch
As the dew-moist grasses parted.
Johnny sank into a crouch
And he sprinkled shining powder
On his beast's enormous head
As the horror sprang toward him
With its eyes a bloody red...

Frightened people in the village
Heard a deep and haunting howl
As the mountain cracked with thunder,
Ending with an eerie growl.
Then, dead silence reeled their senses.
Folks who'd never learned to pray
Found the words to ask one favor–
Make the darkness go away!

With the healing light of morning,
People, fearful of attack,
Stayed inside until they heard the
Shouts of menfolks, coming back.
Wives and children told their stories
But the men had fared the same.
They had started home at midnight,
Fearing that which had no name.

No one knew just what had happened
But they dared not stray too far
'Till, late in the afternoon, a
Little boy name Billy Starr
Came a'running to his mama,
Crying uncontrollably.
He'd found something by the river–
Something everyone should see.

Men reloaded heavy rifles.
No one would be left behind
And they made a brave procession,
Each one dreading what he'd find.
Near the bridge's south embankment,
Seared into the emerald moss
Was an old pouch, made of deerskin,
And the outline of a cross.

The Battle of Feather Creek

Way back in the Ozark mountains
Was a place called Feather Creek
And everybody got along;
At least, all through the week.
But soon as Sunday rolled around,
The arguments grew hot
'Cause half the folks were Baptist
And the other half were not.

Cletus Parker made some money
Working down in Selbyville,
And he left five hundred dollars
To the village in his will.
They already had a tavern
And a picture show combined
So they thought to build a church house
But they didn't say what kind.

Colin Simms donated lumber.
Everything was going fine
'Till Wanella Cole remembered
That a church must have a sign.
Well, that started up a ruckus
'Cause the Baptists all agreed
That the sign should bear their slogan,
But the others disagreed.

Through the fire and smoke that followed
Came a small but frenzied voice:
"Let the church that's got the most members
Be the one to make the choice!"
Toby Brown swore he was neutral
So they let him take the count,
But when all the votes were counted,
Both sides had the same amount.

They were stumped till Monroe Walker
Came up with a foolproof test:
To the choir that sang the loudest
And the longest and the best
Would belong the right to chisel
Their church name upon the sign.
They agreed to meet next Sunday
By the creek at half past nine.

Everybody fried a chicken.
Someone brought some lemonade
And the singers faced each other
While Jim Mackelhaney prayed.
Then, both factions started singing:
"Rock of Ages, cleft for me";
"I'm a poor wayfaring stranger";
"Just a closer walk with Thee."

"Amazing grace, how sweet the sound"
Rang through the summer land
While butterflies redeemed themselves
And all the ladies fanned.
Suddenly, young Timmy Wheeler
Made a loud, prophetic claim.
"Ma, these folks all say they're different
But the songs are just the same!"

Mockingbirds filled in the silence.
Everybody hung his head
For they realized the meaning
In the words that he had said...
If you're driving through the Ozarks,
There's a church you've got to see
For the sign above the doorway
Blazons CHURCH OF HARMONY!